Y0-CZM-699

TIME TO LIVE

Poetry

by
Andrew Stallsmith

Many thanks to Donna Jackson Typesetting for the design and layout.

SON-RISE

Son-Rise Publications
143 Greenfield Road
New Wilmington, PA 16142
1-800-358-0777
ISBN 0-936369-70-1
Printed in the USA

To
Betty Jane
Who shares the time
of my life with
patience, love and grace

THANKS

Giving thanks must begin with God, the Giver of all. After Him, we should thank our ancestors who gave us our genetic and cultural heritage. To our parents, we owe our birth, nurture and upbringing, our ability to love and to accept love.

My parents gave me a large family of brothers and sisters from whom I early learned survival arts in human relationships. I give thanks for family.

In the larger community I have received so much help from so many people, there is no place to begin and no space to list them all. I say only that I will be eternally grateful to "all who have gone into my making."

Having said this, I want to mention four people without whom the making of this book would have been, if not impossible, then extremely difficult for me.

Thanks to Kathleen Davison, who insisted on "having the pleasure" (despite my fear of imposing) of typing and helping to arrange the manuscript.

Thanks to Florence Biros, who, with patient good humor at my ignorance, led me gently by the hand through the intricate maze of publishing.

Thanks to Charles Waugaman, a fellow servant, for the generous sharing of advice from his store of expertise and experience.

To encourage is to: "stimulate," "embolden," and "hearten," to: "impart a spirit of courageous and optimistic resolution and hope needed to continue or persevere." There is one who has done all these things for me, and more. My special thanks to Evelyn Minshull, that Encourager of Writers to whom so many of us owe so much.

Andy

CONTENTS

LIFETIME 11
MOTHER WALKED TO CHURCH 12
PATTERNED 13
REVELATION 14
THE HERITAGE 15
RITE OF PASSAGE 16
BAKERY 17
BELT BUCKLE HIGH 18
WHIPPOORWILL 19
AT RISK 20
THE OLD BARN 21
STARK SENTINEL TREE 22
KILLDEER 23
TINY AUGUST POND 24
AUTUMN EVENING 25
PUMP 25
AUTUMN CHORE 26-27
VIGILANTE 28
GEISHA MAN 29
AUTHORITY 30
AGE 30
WAITING 31
THE MANAGER 32
TO KATHRYN ON HER BIRTHDAY 33
YOU WENT BEFORE ME 34
AND A QUESTION 35
SEEKER 36
TURNING POINT 37

SCULPTORS 38
TO COME ALIVE 39-40
PAST TENSE 41
MEDITATION 42
REPRISAL 43-44
GUILT 44
AFTERMATH.................................. 45
RECOVERY 45
MOMENT OF TRUTH 46-48
GOOD FRIDAY, 1985 49
LIFTED UP..................................... 49
I DO NOT KNOW 50
GOLGOTHA 51
FINISHED 52
WHAT HAS GOD DONE? 52
WHAT CAN I SAY? 53-54
HE LIVES 54
EASTER CROSS 55
BETHLEHEM EVENT 56-60
JOSEPH'S WORD 60
ONLY A SAVIOR 61
UNTO THE LEAST OF THESE........... 61
ANGELS' SONG 62
DONKEY'S WORD 62
MARKED 63-64
PRAYERS — SHE ISN'T SPEAKING ... 65
PRAYERS — HIS CHILDREN 65
PRAYERS — THEY LIVE WITHIN...... 66
PRAYERS — HE BROUGHT A PRESENT 66
PRAYERS — HE IS SO HAPPY 67
PRAYERS — HE IS TOUGH............. 67
PRAYERS —HE DRINKS TOO MUCH 68
DIVINE COMMONPLACE 68

THE LION TAMER 69
A TRUER TELLING 70
THINGS YOU ARE TO ME 71
PAS DE DEUX 71
AT LOSS 72
YESTERDAY 72
COMMON BOND 73
THE PARTING 73
A POEM 74
BEYOND 74
A SMALL BOOK OF POEMS 75
ALONE 76
BUBBLES 77
GENESIS 77
TO LUCKY 78
HORSEPOWER 78
PROGRESS 79
PROGRESS II 80-81
EPOCH 82-83
AT HAYING 84-86
HEIRLOOM 87-88
PURPLE 88
REPRIEVE 89-91
GERONTOLOGY 92
FINITY 92
END OF ALL BEGINNINGS 93
RECYCLED 94
MAY I RECALL 95
GRACEFUL EXIT 97

ACKNOWLEDGEMENTS

"I Do Not Know," "Golgotha," "Lifted Up," "Finished," "What Has God Done," "What Can I Say," and "He Lives," first appeared in "Abingdon's Easter Recitations," copyright 1985, compiled by Evelyn Minshull. Used by permission.

"Only A Savior" and "Unto The Least Of These," first appeared in "Abingdon's Christmas Recitations," copyright 1985, compiled by Evelyn Minshull. Used by permission.

"Alone," "Marked," "Patterned," and "Revelation," first appeared in "Time Of Singing," edited by Charles Waugaman. Used by permission.

"Easter Cross" first appeared in the "United Methodist Reporter."

"Mother Walked to Church," "The Heritage," and "Progress," first appeared in "Church Programs For All Seasons," copyright 1987 by Abingdon Press, written and compiled by Evelyn Minshull. Used by permission.

"Bethlehem Event," "Donkey's Word," "Angel's Song," and "Joseph's Word," first appeared in Abingdon's "Christmas Pageants and Plays," copyright 1990, compiled/edited by Evelyn Minshull. Used by permission.

LIFE TIME

Time for work
and
Time for dreaming
Time to watch
a
Pale cloud streaming
Transient soul
through
An infinite sky
Time to live
Time to die.

In the seventieth year of my life, I look back with profound gratitude, to God, who has given me the time and times of my life. I look forward in faith and in joyous anticipation to timeless living in his presence.

MOTHER WALKED TO CHURCH

Our mother walked to church
Three miles.
In sunshine and in rain
Through mud and snow
She drew us with her.

Tall, saintly, patient
Sundays without end she walked
And we walked too.
We sang, committed memory verses,
Learned sweet Jesus' name.

We followed
Far as we could
And wait
To follow home again.

PATTERNED

My father paced the soft June twilight
Through a field of pale green corn,
Leaned in contented reverie
Upon the stake and rider fence.
I tried to follow in his steps
But had to leap and leap
From one into the next.

That childish game I played
Across the fertile, dew-wet field.
When I came to the fence, he smiled.
"You'll grow," he said.
"Someday you'll be big as me
And have boys of your own."

Sure enough, I grew
And worked and walked
Beside him in the field--
Tried to match him stroke for stroke.
But somehow, even to the day he died
I could not do more work than he--
Or let him know I could.

REVELATION

Our father shaved his mustache once.
We hardly knew him
But crept about to eye the strangeness
Of that patch of smooth grey stubble
Where the mustache should have been.

It seemed as though some stranger
Had taken residence
Within our father's clothes
And there usurped his place in space
Complete with voice and mannerisms.

Our mother smiled enigmatically
And glanced coquettishly
From out the corners of her eyes
To add to all the strangeness.

We hadn't known them well at all.
These two we thought were ours
Had changed before our very eyes,
Become two other people
Who belonged only to themselves
Or rather, to each other.

THE HERITAGE

He never said "I love you,"
Nor did I
The code somehow forbade it
But in the years we worked the land together
There passed between us
A message lovelier than words

That spoke of loyalty and duty and respect
Reverence for the earth and all things live
Honor, trust and faithfulness;
This was the message that he had to give.

He never said "I love you," yet
In all the days I knew him
He spoke no ill of any man
Nor scorned a neighbor
Nor demeaned himself belittling others.

I learned somehow that love
Is living the best way you know how
Giving of yourself when someone needs
And caring for your own with sacrifice.

He never said "I love you," not in words
But said it every day by caring
What I saw him do and heard him say.
And so I do not need to say the words
To pass the message on unto his grandsons.

RITE OF PASSAGE

We used to knee and elbow
Through the pipe
That drained the schoolyard
Underneath the road.

On bravado, dares, and panic
We plunged through
That claustrophobic passage
Into peer respect.

I stuck once
Halfway through
And wonder...

If the status that men seek--
Torn and bleeding talents
Broken to the quick--
Is worth
The reoccurring terrors of the night.

BAKERY

We used a can lid for a mold
Turned out loaves to bake
Upon a sun-hot shingle.

Egg yolk mud--
Squished between our fingers,
Scabbed wrists and ankles--
Made satisfying patties.

We refined the system later,
As all good bakers do...
Frosted some
With elderberry blossoms
Carved feather patterns
In the tops of others.

Our children
Have their Baker Place
In a hollow chestnut stump.
They run ahead to set up shop.

We place our orders
In very grown-up fashion
Choose solemnly between
A luscious pastry
And a piquant pie.
They are good bakers, too.

BELT BUCKLE HIGH

Belt buckle high
In a Thanksgiving kitchen...
Laughter and chatter
Sift down from above
Where cousins play catch-up.
Solemn-eyed babies
Peer down from towers
Of motherly love.

Cranberry rubies
Glitter in gelatin;
Gold-crusted bird
Wafts onion and sage;
Pumpkin pies wink
Through freckles of cinnamon.
Eight and a half
Is just the right age.

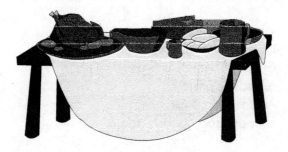

WHIPPOORWILL

Summer twilight sibilance
Sounding from the swing-tree
Too near my boyhood window
Rouses nameless terrors
Stirs an unknown instinct.

"When whippoorwills call,"
The old adage says,
"You may go barefoot..."
Free to run lightfoot
Through sunsweet meadows
Wade among tadpoles
Scare water skippers.

Whippoorwills' answer
Softened by distance
Sounds with sweet urgency
Faint melancholy:
All life is waiting
You're free to go.

AT RISK

"Play for keeps?"
I would not play for keeps.
My marbles were too precious
Too hard won, to risk the loss
Of even one within the ring
Of hard-packed earth.
In passionate possessiveness
I clutched my meager hoard
And backed away.

"Play for keeps?"
I would not play for keeps.
The talents just discovered
In my young manhood years
Were much too fragile yet, to risk
Within that ring of hard-packed earth
Where men still play their games
Of get and keep.

"Play for keeps?"
I had to play for keeps
For time was running on
And would not wait for safer games.
The risk, once taken, proved
To be an end within itself.
I lost.
But now I cannot wait
To find another game.

THE OLD BARN

The old barn stands in weathered disarray
In weary stoicism slanting
Aged, brittle bones laid bare and roof a prey
To storm's wild ranting.

Scant shelter the ruined shell provides
The North wind's icy blasts invade
Once-snug precincts, and drifted snow piles high
Where newborn foal and calf once played.

Then proud and new, these rotting beams
Rejoiced the man whose steady care
In quiet faithfulness and happy toil
Had put them there.

Each brace and purlin, rafter, joist, and plate
So much himself contained
Both faced with confidence and steadfast strength
What time and fate ordained.

Both now are past, their times outgrown
But on a bright May morning
One still may sense a quiet presence near
Or hear a trace chain jingle without warning.

STARK SENTINEL TREE

Stark sentinel tree, bared to the bone
Lone guardian of a hedgerow choked with brush
How stubbornly you cling to earth
Although immune to seasons' alchemy.

The winds with which your lissome limbs
Once danced in graceful arabesques
Among their stiffened stubs
Now sough a dirge.

The downwind upstarts you had sown
Year after patient year in profligate fecundity--
  Who might a copse of progeny have grown
  To shade your final resting place,
  Probe with gentle roots your moldering form,
  And make you live again within their lives--
Year after dreadful year succumbed
To sickle bar and plow.

That husbandman who cultivates
The graveyard of your young
Will come with howling teeth
To section up your trunk
And haul you to an alien resting place
Where you will render up upon his hearth
The suns of many seasons.

KILLDEER

Where cowpath crosses brook
Seemed the perfect place
To brood your eggs
Until the cattle came.

Great lumbering engines
In placid cavalcade
Serenely on a hundred cloven hooves
Tread out your fragile treasure.

As you in frantic fluttering
Display your sacrificial ruse
Before incurious eyes

While bits of shattered shell
Swirl softly
Upon the muddy trickle
That slowly heals a hoofprint.

TINY AUGUST POND

Tiny August pond
Green algae-scummed, weed-prisoned
Passive, basking, indolent
You lie in time-suspended wisdom,
Immune alike
To midday sun's oppressive glare
Cicada's penetrating drill
And my impotent gaze.

Your inscrutable facade
Compels strange fascination.
As dementia's vacant stare
Conceals its dreadful wisdom
And blinded eyes betray
No trace of thought behind them
So your self-protecting veil
Hides answers
To questions
I don't know how to ask.

AUTUMN EVENING

I walked abroad one misty autumn evening
And saw a patch of sunlight on the ground
A spot of brightness that belied
The darkening sky and early dusk
And teased my senses into pleased surprise.

Then I saw the tree from which it fell.
The summer's sun in pieces one by one
Had laid a golden carpet on the green
A valiant challenge to the coming night
And left the stark dark branches to their rest.

PUMP

Ka-loomp-chunk, ka-loomp-chunk
Through faerie soft evenings of spring.
Ka-loomp-chunk, ka-loomp-chunk
In brutal, bitter, barren, winter.

Ka-loomp-chunk, ka-loomp-chunk
"Spring water never freezes."
Ka-loomp-chunk, ka-loomp-chunk
Cool and sweet on summer-thirsty lips.
Ka-loomp-chunk, ka-loomp-chunk
Water for gardens, water for cattle
Water for dishes, water for bathing
Taken for granted, water of life.

AUTUMN CHORE

He was rolling pumpkins
Down the hill.
A strange and wasteful act,
I thought,
And paused as if to question...
Then saw the situation.

They were old,
With Halloween long past.
Some sagged upon themselves
In quiet desperation.

After one wild fling at glory
The gully's brushy bottom
Received them into rest.

These unchosen ones
Doomed to uselessness
When gleeful childish fancy
Passed them by
Never chanced to grin
In fiendish fire
Upon some porch or windowsill
Or better yet to grace a winter table
Redolent with spice
And festive fowl displayed.

He'd been told to clear them out
And took the easy way
As we are wont to do.
And who's to say that
Bounding, headlong crash Into oblivion
Was not preferred
Against a wheelbarrow trundle
To the compost heap?

In sullen autumn twilight
He had changed a half hour's drudgery
Into a game of "See how far they go"
Never dreaming of
Next summer's hillside
Rioting in green and gold.

VIGILANTE

Ike scoured his fields
Searching out weeds
Hoe cocked
In attack position
Ropey sinews taut
Beneath bronze skin.

"Let one weed grow,
A million others come
To keep it company."

An upwind neighbor
Let his thistles seed.
Ike raged
To see the tiny
Paratroop invasion.
He shook his fist
And vowed retaliation.

GEISHA MAN

Geisha man
Hobbling on irrelevant emotions
Mindbound
In ties of outmoded custom
Crammed
Into constricting molds of preconceptions
Coerced into conformity
Used to serve another's purpose.

Spiritual cripple
Who cannot thrive in strength and purpose
As life and living challenge every faculty...
Cannot grow in truth and substance
In the ebb and flow of fortune
To leap on healthy feet toward the dawn
Welcoming with expectant arms
The future truth.

Tottering helplessly in prescribed circles
Of meaningless rote
In desperate awareness or smug complacency
You have left your children unbound and free
And now, by these liberated children
Are being swept headlong
Into a future
With which you cannot cope.

AUTHORITY

The master trails his whip
Behind him in the dust
As slowly he advances
Upon his cowering slave.

No need to brandish openly
The symbol of his power.

His control is absolute
To make his wishes known
With but a glance or nod
He orders life and death.

AGE

Old and bent
He stands in fumble fashion
Engaged in "trying to remember."
Faded eyes turned inward
Head half-cocked
Great bony hands splayed out
As if to catch a thought
And force it bodily
Into obedience
He hangs immobilized by mental effort
Upon the precipice of consciousness.
And then, at last aware
Of others waiting for an answer
Says, "But that was long ago
And of no interest now."

WAITING

She sings
In quavering soprano
Furrowed face alight
With praise and adoration
Faded chicory eyes
Fixed on the cross.

Teardrops pick their way
Unheeded down
The parchment page
Where care and joy
In equal measure
Are written large.

She sits alone
Attending to the sermon.
Alone she hears
The benediction given.
When greeted by the pastor
At the door, she smiles
A gentle smile
And longs for heaven.

THE MANAGER

She walked beside him
But slightly to the rear
A little brown hen of a woman
Content to scurry in his wake
Fluff up his ego as need be--
While he, the lordly male,
Drove onward.

It had paid her well,
For he had been successful
Beyond their wildest dreams.

Now he is gone
Carried off by one or other
Of the ills
Lordly males are heir to.

"Poor thing," they say, "poor thing,
How will she manage?"

TO KATHRYN ON HER BIRTHDAY

Another year; and just for you
On your own day, a word or two:

When daily work and care are done,
Time to relax and feel the sun;
Its midday strength is mellowed now,
Diffused and softer, yet somehow
More valuable as evening nears.

And so one's life with added years
Becomes enhanced. With duty done
And cares aside, the race is run
More gently now, with time to see
The tapestry the years have spun.

With undiminished zest you go
About your days--a joy to know.

Happy Birthday Happy Birthday Happy Birthday

YOU WENT BEFORE ME

You went before me.
Not so old in years
As in experience
You tasted life
And spat some out--
"Unpalatable," you said.

You dreamed a life
The way a life should be
Nor accepted less of it
Though losing much
That might have been enjoyed.

When night descended
You saw with your heart's eyes
A clearer truth
Than any light had shown.

When death came sweeping past
You called him friend
And entered gladly in his train.

AND A QUESTION

Do you suppose
That through the ever-rolling surge
Of human history
A thread of Reason runs?

    Nameless terrors prowl
    The ignorance-shrouded corners of the mind.
    Relentlessly, unanswered questions wheel,
    Sure of their time.
    Soul-thirst fever squats
    Remorselessly upon life's shoulders.

Or is Reason just a trick
We play upon ourselves
For fear of being left
Alone
With God?

SEEKER

This animated lump of clay
In fineness formed
By creation's gracious act
Lives beyond imagining.

Bound each to each
In quest of meaning
Flesh and spirit mingle
In mystic co-dependence

Peer up and out
In poignant hope
Plunge down and in
In search of verities,

While off the splintered surface
Dance and glance
Prismatic overtures
Beckoning
In all directions.

TURNING POINT

Within a life
A line of demarcation drawn
Approached unwitting by degrees
Arrived at finally
In instantaneous awareness

Is not so much a physical delineation
But more a change
In the complexion of the land
Once known--observed--and passed
Is absolute
Forever after fixed against return.

One may look back in wonder
At the child who journeyed there
In the armor of his ignorance
But dare not grieve in mourning
For things that never were...

Instead, made vulnerable
By newfound insight,
Must turn in resolution
To face an unknown land.

SCULPTORS

The NOW
The present moment
Caught between
The perfide past
And devious future
Lies
In pristine acquiescence.

More than just a sheet
On which we limn
The perceived vision
Of our lives,

Rather a stone
Which our repeated acts
Have worn and grooved
And yet left free
Of final judgment,

Patiently accepting
Each moment's minute etching
Until such time as now shall cease
And past, alone, remain
The finished image
Of our lives.

TO COME ALIVE

March, raucous month
Harsh as crows' returning call
Changeling child of two seasons
Your boisterous winds impose
Tumultuous tyranny.

As tuning forks arouse
The sympathetic strings
So do your wild persistent gusts
Excite the soul to desperate yearnings.

Winter's stoic pattern of survival
So long endured with frozen patience
Gives way to wrenching hope.
Is it as hard for trees to wake?

To fell that first great burning surge
Of stinging sap
Drawn by a burgeoning sun
Up, up through winter-shrunken pores?

Are daffodils in their dark beds
Of death-like slumber
Loath to awake, to start again
The hectic, painful task of living?

And crocuses, those bright and jaunty
Harbingers of spring,
Do they sometimes malinger--
Reluctant to begin another season?

You grant a short reprieve to living
In spates of returned winter
To all but snowdrops,
Those heirs of ancient discipline,
Who needs must bloom beneath the snow.

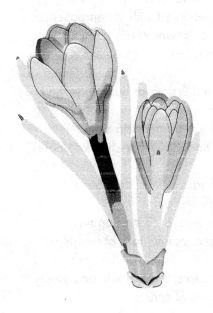

PAST TENSE

A scarce perceived yearning
Steals across my consciousness
Unbidden and unwelcome.

Some nostalgic dinosaur
From out my own prehistory
Intrudes its awkward presence
Demanding recognition.

I was not me yet then,
Having only lately come
To be myself.

But one must draw his past behind him
Bound by strands of gossamer
Strong as steel,
To all that's gone into his making.

One might fain shed his past
As serpents shed their strictive skins
And come all shining new into the present
Relieved at once of ancient obligations.

Only robots
Forever destined to remain precisely as created
Spring full-grown into the present
To function at a stated phase of evolution.
But we
Being rooted in the compost of our pasts
Must deal with dinosaurs
As well as space ships.

MEDITATION

I think of dark complexities
Filtering through
The matrix of my life and times.
I think of far horizons beyond which
The mind gropes, seeking for verities.

I think of nostalgic beckonings
From out the past
Laying claim to the present.
I think of ideals,
Once clear and bright,
Now faded into commonplace expediency.
I think of time, stretching to infinity,
Encapsuled into hours and days and lifetimes.
I think of life, and love and joy,
Disappointments, pain and sorrow,
And know that it is good.

REPRISAL

What alchemy bestirs my soul
These sun balmed days of spring?
Nostalgia's knife is driven deep
And twisted....

Sweet pain engulfs my winter-weary heart
Memories flood every sense
Of years gone by
When life was young.
Every spring was lived
As if a million more were waiting
Just for my felicity.

Through perfumed days
Light and shadow, clouds and wind
Were playthings.
Every flower blooming bloomed for me.
Every secret, sun-warmed spot
Awaited my discovery.
All of creation catered to my pleasure.

But memories are not enough
To satisfy the heart's deep yearning.
Each present moment must be lived
And living treasured.

And if the care-scarred heart
And if the guilt-encrusted soul
Are not so quickly moved
To splendor?

Be glad for that which moves at all
And cherish it.
For without movement,
Pain or pleasure,
Life becomes a stagnant pool
Immune to living--
The anteroom of death.

GUILT

A dark and sullen, knowing eye
Floats evilly upon the tide
Of hovering memories,
Held numbly in abeyance
By some sheer act of will
That saps the strength for living.

Apathy becomes the rule
That governs life.
To care would broach the dikes
That hold reality at bay
And let the whelming flood
Wash out existence.

AFTERMATH

The song is ended
  Why do you keep on playing?

The race is won
  Why do you keep on running?

When no one needs
  Why do you keep on giving?

When life is done
  Why do you keep on living?

RECOVERY

A crazed glass mirror
Hanging in a barren room
Reflects a fractured image.

A neighbor's guarded look reveals
A cautious sympathy.

Deep within a loved one's eyes
Tender compassion, and accepting love
Begin their healing task.

MOMENT OF TRUTH

I slept
I woke
I slept again
Or did not sleep
I cannot know.

But in some half-remembered state
Of fancy, acquiescent
To nebulous ideas and effervescent notions
Unacceptable to incredulous reason
And wholly pleasant,
I drifted.

With uncritical acceptance
I gradually perceived a Presence.
I spoke, no, did not speak
I merely thought, *Who are you?*
I did not hear;
I simply felt the answer,
Come.

Swiftly then
On silent wings we lifted
Through boundless realms of time and space
To some far place....
Or was it near at hand,
With but an opaque curtain drawn
Between it and the farthest reaches
Of the conscious mind?

We came at last to some fair field
Of curious wonder.
We moved through paths of beauty unalloyed,
With plants and trees so exquisitely tended
A loving care was manifest
On every side.

In awe-filled fascination
I turned inquiring eyes
To my companion
Who proclaimed quietly what I
Had only half-dared to surmise:
"The garden of the Lord,"
And to my unasked question answered,
"Aye, the souls of man."

They stood in groves
Well-tended and serene:
Some veritable giants,
Some of stripling growth,
Some gnarled and twisted,
Ingrown upon themselves.

But there were open spaces, too.
When I inquired
The Voice
With matchless sadness said,
"These never grew."

As on we moved
I bolder grew
And knew contempt and scorn
For all the stunted, twisted ones.

"With all the care
With all the infinite loving care
They have," I said,
"Surely they could grow
Much better than they do!

Observe that poor misshapen thing
In that small open space,
How well the earth is loosed
About its roots,
How moist and rich the humus is.
The ones so near about it
Have grown beautifully.
Surely it could make
Some progress too."

I looked to my companion for agreement
And perhaps some commendation
For my zeal.
I saw instead a look of pity,
A look of such compassion
As I have never known,
A look that pierced my heart
And then I knew....

That wizened, dried-up thing,
Unresponsive to divinest care,
Ungrateful, stunted specimen,
That stubborn, unproductive soul...

Was mine.

GOOD FRIDAY, 1985

All of us have been bitten by the snake--a fatal
wound festering with the venom of disobedience--
selfishness--lust--greed--jealousy--distrust--hate--
This we have in common with every individual who
has ever lived. God--our God--laid aside his glory,
came into our world as one of us to bring the remedy.
He is the remedy--
Jesus said: "As Moses lifted up the serpent in the
wilderness, even so must the Son of man be lifted up"
(John 3:14 KJV)

LIFTED UP

God in human flesh: Immanuel
Perfect flesh, now torn and violated.

    God--come down to us
    In seeking love
    Now lifted up by us in agony.

We look upon him and he draws
The poison from the serpent's sting
Heals us, and makes us whole.

On this very day, nearly 2,000 years ago, he died
that we might live. Believers have ever stood in awe at
this transcendent deed of mercy, grace, and love.

I DO NOT KNOW

I do not know
I cannot tell
Why He should brave
The gates of hell
For me--for me
His weakest friend.

I only know
That once he died
To kill my sins
And stem the tide
Of guilt--of guilt
That prisoned me.

Now I am free
He paid the price
With His own life
God's sacrifice
Of love--of love
That ransomed me.

A very personal thing--a very Individual thing. We
may say he died for all mankind--but each of us must
know in his deepest heart of hearts, HE DIED FOR ME.

GOLGOTHA

Yes, I was there that fateful day
The day they took our Christ away
To that dark hill of pain.

My sin increased the pain he bore
Made sharp the crown of thorns he wore
And drove the nails home.

"Father, forgive them," now he prays
The dying sun extends its rays
To touch his anguished face.

"Forgive them" from his loving heart
Streams of Grace and Mercy start
To overcome the world.

Yes, I was there the day he died
My sin with him was crucified
And I am ever his.

When one responds to Christ, his life is changed--the
world's a different place--there is hope--there is peace-
-there is joy--even in the midst of problems and troubles.
Even secular history is divided into BC
    (Before Christ) and AD (The year of our Lord).

FINISHED

"It is finished."
From the lips of Him
Made sin for me
That last victorious cry
Announced to all the universe
That from this moment on
His creatures were made free
Of numbing guilt--
Destroying death,
Made free to live
Abundantly.

In that awe-filled day <u>God came close</u>, revealed himself--his nature--more fully than ever before.

WHAT HAS GOD DONE?

Darkness and trembling Earth
A veil is rent
And thus lays bare
The very heart of God:
The seeking, yearning heart of God.

What has God done
But give himself
But give himself in agony
To draw his creatures close,
To draw us close, in Love?

Words fail us--we stand in humble adoration...Charles Wesley wished for a thousand languages in which to express praise to God.

WHAT CAN I SAY?

What can I say
That others have not said
So many times before
To honor Christ,
To magnify his Name?

Each word
A new and perfect jewel
Would not suffice
To laud his sacrifice
And tell his glory.

I can but use
These old words, new to me
Words that he most yearns to hear:
My Lord, I come
I come, to Thee.

I come--Let us say it once again in our hearts--and
let Him draw us close. Let us pray:
Oh God, you who are all love--
You who yearn for the welfare
Of your creatures--we do come
To you today--once again--as far
As our selfishness will let us.
We come--yielding as much of
Ourselves as we can to you.
We come--knowing that you came
The whole way to seek us to save
Us--Draw us, we pray,
Beyond the limitations of our

Selfish fears--beyond our
Appetite for <u>things</u>--Draw
Us into a willingness to
<u>Lose</u> ourselves in your love--
That your life among us--that
Your death upon the cross--
Might not have been in vain
For each of us. We thank you
And praise you--for all you have
Done and continue to do for us.
Make us willing and useful instruments
Of your peace and love. In
Christ's name we pray--Amen

HE LIVES

He lives again!
Go tell the news
Go shout it from the highest hills
Go tell the sin-sick, guilty world
That he who died for you and me
Who took our place upon the tree
Who paid the price to set us free
That Christ, our Savior
Lives again!

EASTER CROSS

We sand the cross
And varnish it
To make it shine
In wood grained beauty.
It glows in candlelight
Against rich velvet.

No splinters here, no knots
To scathe a back
Laid open by the scourge.
No stain of blood, no bits of flesh
Ground by agony
Into the very grain of it.

But that was long ago
And now the golden chalice gleams
And lilies nod in silken splendor.

BETHLEHEM EVENT

I searched...
I scoured this pilgrim-clotted town
For some small space
Some decent place
To lay my loved one down.

She is so weary; I see it in her face
She'll not complain, but sits so patiently
Upon the stoic, faithful beast
Whose jarring gait has helped
To bring her to this place.

I searched...
In desperation I implored
The keeper of the inn for shelter
Any shelter
To shield my precious from the night
And give her privacy.

II

There is no place--unless--
Unless you would be willing--no--
It would not do.
Lambs are born in stables
Foals and cattle, too
But human babies--no--
It would not do.

Better there than in the street,
You say--perhaps--
Perhaps a blanket on a pile of hay
Would do. I'll send my wife.
You see that roofline--There--

By starlight--half set into the bank?
Here--use this gate--
I'll settle with you in the morning.
I have to go. There's much to do.
It's late.

III
You'd better go.
She's just a child herself
Though great with child.
Take a light--you'll need it.
There is a wild look in her eyes
Though outward calm she kept for him.
Go now--I'll see to things.

IV
You say your name is Joseph?
Here, Joe, hold the light--
A little closer. Men generally
Aren't allowed at times like these.
You'll have to do.
None else to call.
I see you've found some hay--
A bed of sorts
This drink of gall wail casc her some.
The labor's started.

There, dear, drink it all.
Here's a blanket roll.
And press down--so--and push!
That's right; hold on to Joe
Squeeze his hand tight--and push!
Soon you can rest.
Groan if you like

No one to hear but us...
Us and the cattle...
They won't care; they're used to pain
And groaning when the pike
Increases their toil.

Push now!--Again!--Ah, there we are.
A fine young man--A son for you, Joe.
I've brought a little water and some oil
You want to wrap him? Good.
I see you've swaddling with you.
You do it well for one so young.
You've practiced, maybe, with a brother
Or a sister. I'll go now--
I have to help the mister.

V

Joseph, dearest Joseph--
Here is the son God promised...
So long ago, it seems, we've lived
A lifetime in nine months.

See how his tiny fingers
Flutter on my breast.
See how he gazes at your face
As if imprinting every line
Upon his consciousness.
Perhaps he feels my love for you, somehow.

You've been so good to me these months--
So patient...and so kind...
No man living could do better
By a wife.

Would you care to hold him
For a little space?
There, he likes it--see how his face
Lights up at yours.
It seems so natural to see him
In your arms.

It's peaceful here...
All quiet and serene.
I'm glad there was no room in town
With all its noise and stir.
Yes, I'll rest now.
You can lay him in that manger
If I should sleep
And you need to lay him down.

VI

You're awake?--I'm sorry.
I've tried to keep them quiet,
But they were so excited.
They've come to see the baby--
Just a group of shepherds
From out upon the hills above the town.

They say they've seen a vision--
A host of heavenly creatures
Winging down from glory
Singing praises unto God and bringing
Messages of peace
To all mankind.

They were told to come...
Told where to find the baby...
Told he would be lying in a manger...
Wrapped in swaddling clothes.

How could they know? Unless--
Unless the dream is true!
I've never doubted--really
But there have been doubts--
I'm only human, after all
And these nine months have taken toll
Of faith.

How gracious is our God!
How condescending
To send these humble ones
To heal my doubts.
But now, if you are able
We'll let them in.

VII

You may come in now.
Step softly, please, the baby sleeps.
Yes, his name is Jesus, and he keeps
Our hearts in love, forever...

JOSEPH'S WORD

A Son!--my son!
Not of my flesh;
No seed of loins--but mine!
To love, to nurture, and to teach.
I share with God
The fathering of his Son,
A precious task.
Lord of heaven, sustain me in it.

ONLY A SAVIOR

Only a tiny baby,
Only a stable dim;
Only the humble shepherds
Were there to worship him.
Only a heavenly chorus,
Proclaiming a holy birth;
Only his own star shining
On the Savior of the earth.

UNTO THE LEAST OF THESE

Not to kings and princes
Not to men of might
Not to lords of righteousness
Was he made known that night.

But to the lowly shepherds
The angels sang their song
And glory shone about them;
They saw the heavenly throng.

Not in a golden palace
Satin pillows for his head
But with wanderers and beggars
Was he to make his bed.

Still to the meek and lowly
The gentle Savior comes.
When humble hearts receive him,
They are his welcome home.

ANGELS' SONG

"Peace on earth!" the angels sang.
"Not peace but a sword," He said.
"For the jealous world will seek your life
Who follow where I led."
"Good will to men," the song declares.
"Thy will be done," He said.
"The bitter cup of death I drink
That all mankind may eat eternal bread."
"Glory to God in the highest!"
We sing with the angel train---
Our broken lives healed by his love;
He has not worked in vain.

DONKEY'S WORD

A baby in MY manger--on hay I need
To fuel my body for the tasks
My master lays upon me.
    A baby claims my manger.
Strangers clamor at the door,
Disturb my rest with foolish tales
Of kings, of angels singing in the sky.
    A baby needs my manger.
No place his own to lay his head;
No down and fleece in love prepared
Receive his precious presence.
    A baby fills my manger
With glory light, surpassing peace,
A burst of joy, a dream of hope....
    Welcome to my manger.

MARKED

My Mother loves to tell me stories;
Stories of myself.
She tells of shepherds, stars, and kings,
Of angels singing in the sky,
Of wondrous gifts, and signs and portents,
A dream she shared with Father.

I love to hear them
Or always have...

What do they mean;
These happenings
That marked my birth?
Shall I let them rule my life
Or are they just the natural products
Of parental fondness?
How can I know?

What is this star-claimed fate
That dogs my life?
Why wasn't I like other boys?
Where does it come from,
This insight, this understanding
I possess, that seemed to leap
Beyond my lessons into depths
I feared to plumb.

I cannot answer.

Meanwhile I work the trade
My Father taught me
And trust the grain of things
To lead me into knowledge.

My wild cousin, John,
Elijah-styled prophet,
Steeped in ancient wisdom,
Preaches in the wilderness.
One day I'll go and hear him.

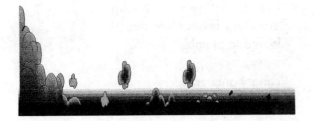

PRAYERS

She isn't speaking to her husband, Lord
I don't know exactly why
She says he doesn't listen anyway
I know he loves her still
And tell her that
But he was raised to think that men
Must never show their feelings.
Please show me how to get them talking
Honestly with one another
And then with you.
You always listen.

PRAYERS

His children
Are a disappointment to him, Lord.
He says they steal and drink and lie.
He is bitter and resentful
Not for what it does to them
But for what it does to him.
How can I tell him
They have just fulfilled his
Real expectations?
How can I tell him that
They learned it all from him?

PRAYERS

They live within the same house, Lord
But scarcely live together
They talk
When household matters must be settled
But otherwise they might as well be strangers.
When they were young
They built a house together
And raised a family and laughed
But now....
Why is it, Lord
They've grown so far apart?

PRAYERS

He brought a present when he came
Whether an excuse for stopping
Or as a kind of bribe, a payment
For something he imagined I
Could get from you on his behalf.
I accepted it with grace.
Oh, help me make him understand
That everything was paid for
In the gift you gave.

PRAYERS

He is so happy to have found you, Lord.
He says that when his wife
Laughed in his face and left
You saw him through.
He teaches his young son your ways
And hopes for better days.
His parents are afraid he is fanatic
And tell him so
But he forgives them all.

PRAYERS

He is tough, Lord.
Oh, he is tough--and stubborn.
He has gone to church all his life
But still he tries to tough it out
Without you.
Help me to help him know
Dependence on your power
Is not a sign of weakness
But of strength.

PRAYERS

He drinks too much
But came to church once
With his wife and children
A cry for help that no one answered.
We were too busy planning schemes
To increase membership
Forgive us, Lord.

DIVINE COMMONPLACE

Who made the sun to rise this morning?
Who gave the dew to the thirsting grasses?
Who made the stars to shine last night?
Who gives us life every day that passes?

Everything that we take for granted
All the small things that make life good
Baby's smile and love's caresses
Beauty and truth for the spirit's food...

In the commonplace and the ordinary
His steadfast love for us he shows.
Our God is a God of simple things;
Heaven comes to us in everyday clothes.

THE LION TAMER

I have a lion lives in me
I shelter him though I would not.
He lives in me, feeds on my will,
Influences each act and thought.

I try to stare him down to prove
Myself the master: Mind over brute
Alas! too late, his sullen strength
Has grown too great! Ah bitter truth.

But there is One--oh there is One
Who comes when called by name
And with His clear cool gaze of righteousness
All my puny effort shames.

Myself--my lion--cowers now
I in my Savior's Presence--free
Must needs give Him myself, but lo
He gives my own self back to me.

A TRUER TELLING

When I was young and impudent
The words, "I love you"
Rolled glibly off my tongue.
I used the words
To court your favor
Full knowing the effect they had.

Too easy words, too quickly spoken
Used for selfish ends.
I did not know yet then
What love could mean.

Now I am old
And have some sense of honesty
I hesitate to say the words
But rather try
To let my actions show my caring
Even though my deeds
Fall woeful short
Of their imposing task.

THINGS YOU ARE TO ME

A presence in the night
A place to warm my feet
A stake to hold my tether
And guide me safely back.

Assurance--comfort--quietness
A wall of certainty off which
To bounce my questing ball
Companion, confidante, and friend,
Lover.

PAS DE DEUX

You give me hours of my life--
You have some claim to after all--
To use as I see fit,

To nurture muse, pander to duty
And follow joy's sweet supplications,
Tracing the unchosen path
Of least persistence.

Inexorable time herds us before
Its halloing vanguard,
Nips in effortless pursuit.

While we together dance
Our daily pirouette
In solemn acquiescence.

AT LOSS

I reached across the void
That separated us
And you reached too.
We had no way of knowing, really
How far we were apart.

If we should touch
Would you know then
That we belong together?

I reached and stretched and thought
That we might bridge the gap
With words
But you lost interest and wandered off.

YESTERDAY

You saw me from your window
And you waved.
My heart leaped up
The day became worth living
And I ran
To be sooner where you were.
I waited
But you never came.

COMMON BOND

She stands
In acquiescence slightly bowed
Before him
Prisoner of common usage.

Her eyes--
He cannot see their burning gaze
Directed at his feet.

He cannot know the truth
In them revealed
If they should meet his own.

And just as well--
He could not bear the truth she knows.
He stands complacently
Prisoner of common usage.

THE PARTING

Our bags all packed,
We said goodby
With mien of calm composure
Dearly won.

We shook each other's hands
In lieu of deadly weapons
And wished each other well...

We lied.

A POEM

A poem, like a flash flood,
Comes raging out of the sub-conscious
Overflows the banks of everyday existence
Gouges and scours
The dry bed of mundane activities
Gathers material for its expression.

Overpowering in its urgency
Crested with aborted dreams and uprooted ideas
Casts fond notions up on barren shoals
Leaves a shambles of smug complacencies
Spends itself in the intricate effort
Of words.

BEYOND

Love in June, good-bye
Familiar tune, good-bye
Sweet afternoon, good-bye
Orphaned spittoon.

Nonsense is relevant.
Where did the yellow went?
Meanwhile I pitch my tent
Across the abyss.

Did you dare come to me
No more alive--but free!
Together we could see
Far into night.

A SMALL BOOK OF POEMS

I met her in a book
Last night
And fell in love.

She showed me all her heart
And bravely spread her treasures out
For all the world to see
As well as me.

Her love of life
Her gallant spirit's power
Touched a sympathetic chord
And drew us close.

We met and shared
A moment intimate
As only heart and mind can share;
Sweet understanding flashed between us.

And if we never meet
And if she never knows that I exist,
What matters that?
I have her dowry.

ALONE

I heard the peepers keen tonight
Beneath a gentle April rain.
Their strident piping scathed
A wound new-healed.

So many times I've heard them
Nestled snug
Against your beating heart.

We listened for them, you and I
Through springs uncounted.
In new love and in old
They never failed us.

Tonight they kept their date,
Chimed a hymn to love...
But in my lonely ears
They shrilled a dirge.

BUBBLES

An elephant named...Bubbles?
A light and airy name
Seeming to float
Above her squat and ugly body.

The children loved her
And would stroke the coarse black hair
That scraggled sparsely
Over leathery gray skin.

She was just a baby and would grow
And did--into a ponderous hulk
That shuffled endlessly
In caged boredom--cadging peanuts.

GENESIS

Telltale trails
Silvery snails' tracks
Leading back
Link us
To the place
Of our beginnings.

TO LUCKY

I would not ask you to gallop now,
To race the wind as we once did
When you were much younger than I.

I am older now, but you are much older.
I can not spare you pain
At the expense
Of hurting you by walking.

We both know that soon
You will be
Unable to carry me
I think we both know
That then
I will not ride again.

HORSEPOWER

Black pistons slamming icy earth
Surging power in fluid motion
Breaking the psychic barrier
Of known entities
Bursting into reality.

PROGRESS

They came and straightened out the brook
And drained the pools
Where devil's darning needles
(If you tell a lie they sew your mouth shut)
Darted their iridescent stitchery
Through boyhood's timeless afternoons
Beneath a sapient sun.

Men walk dryshod where once
Toads' tapioca-stranded nursery puddles stood
Where lowly crawdads
Reared their mud-tiered towers
And peepers shrilled their mating songs
To usher in another spring.

"We need the land," they said,
"To feed a hungry world.
Skunk cabbage will not fill an empty belly.
We must wrestle with the earth
To make her yield her bounty."
While down below they built a dam
That flooded half a county.

PROGRESS II

Two centuries ago a grieving husband
Chose this peaceful spot
In which to bury his life's love.

A chestnut guardian
Visible from any field
He left in charge
And went about his daily tasks
In stoical acceptance.

His pensive gaze, alone
Drawn to that lonely sentinel
From field work or chores
Betrayed his suffering.

In that high corner of his farm
With slope toward the east
He joined her later on.

Others brought their cherished dead
To that fair place for final rest
And were not turned away
But given space to lay them.

The gentle hillside flowered many summers
And many winters weathered its dull stones
Its tranquil sameness undisturbed.

The mall was built
In half a dozen months;
The tiny graveyard had no deed
And no one to defend it.

The guardian chestnut
Long ago succumbed to time
And joined its charges
In the earth.

Concrete and macadam sealed the earth
No winter's snow or summer's sun
Can touch its living face.

It lies in sterile barrenness
Beneath the tread of commerce.

EPOCH

One there was
Who stood astride this hill
Imposed his will
With little more than axe and oxen...

Whose bliss was toil
On land he called his own
To dress and serve unstintingly.
He owned the land
The land owned him
A covenant of co-indenture.

His axe at once hewed out a home
And cleared a porridge field.

Well-versed in self-reliant arts
And settlers' lore
He took himself to be
The husbandman of all creation.

His shovel taught a wayward brook
To square a field
Drained a sour bog
And dug a dornic out.

No idle moment was allowed
To rob him of a task well done.

Among his other crops he grew
Three stalwart sons
Who trod his footsteps in the soil
Steeped in his ways--
Lived out their days
In unremitting servitude
Bound to the land
In ways they could not understand
With worn-out wives
Who shared their helplessness.

Their children and their children's children
Fled the farm
Now hold the heritage
For recreation.
Some mystic bondage
Draws them back
To sleep where grandsir's spirit
Haunts their guilty freedom.

The untilled land
Now slips by stages back
Through goldenrod, blackberry and aspen
To groves of thigh-sized maple.
Stonewalls and dead-furrows
Arrow their way
Through dappled stillness.

One who knows to look
May yet discover
A twist of wire
Clinging to a faithful post
Relics of a time outgrown

AT HAYING

I saw them running in the field
My husband and my son
In crazy, broken, erratic dashes.
The field was nearly mown.

I watched them from my sink-window
One smaller boy and one grown tall.
Some manic game of tag they played.
The tractor idled on, forgotten.

I saw their quarry then,
A tiny animated speck it was,
Dive frantically beneath
A new-mown windrow.

My son (he's twelve years old and quick)
Leaped and clutched a mound of grass.
A thin scream, carried on the soft June air,
Pierced...like shards of ice.

Untangling a small body from the hay
He handed it, still screaming, to his father
One swift blow,
The screaming stopped.

I am farm-bred and know
The ways of life
And death
Inherent in that life.

And yet that piercing cry
Of purest terror
Clung to my consciousness
As frigid iron clings
To moisture-laden skin.

Predators!
The word blazed sharp
Unbidden to my mind.
Revulsion welled within my heart.
I turned away in sorrow.

I laid the table then
For it was nearly noon.
My unaccustomed brusqueness broke
The handle from a favored jelly dish.

The tractor comes into the yard and stops.
I hear them talking quietly
As they approach the house.

These are my men!
The men I love more dearly
Than even life, itself.
My heart melts in forgiveness,
Forgiveness for something
They cannot know they've done.

They come and stand before me
And my son speaks
Through huskiness of unshed tears:
"Mom, a little rabbit got its legs cut off,
We had to kill it...."

His manner solemn as befits a man
Who's forced by circumstance
To do the right and dreadful thing.

I weep for him
Or weep on his behalf,
For he is nearly man
And men are not allowed
The balm of healing tears.

I lay my hand upon his shoulder
(He allows me that) and say
The best I can for him.
"I'm sorry it happened, son,
But you have done
What any good and self-respecting man
Would surely have to do."

They nod together solemnly,
Go out to wash the blood off of their hands
And come to lunch.

HEIRLOOM

This old song your Aunt Hannah wrote
Contains wailing in general
And enough morals to float a Sunday School.

Pa was so proud of her;
Carved every word, he did
In Tulip Wood
One verse to a block.

Hinged them all together, ingenious like
So's they'd all stack neat on top o' one another.

See how when you pick one up
The rest all sort o' flip-flop
Into their places below
So's to make the purtiest wall hangin'.

Felt so bad when she died
He couldn't bear to look at it no more
Couldn't even stand to hear the words.

Left them all stacked up together
In the loft--I fell heir to it.
It don't seem right nohow to sell it.

There ain't no room to take it
Where I'm goin'.

Maybe one of your young'uns
Would like it--when they're grow'd a little...
It don't take up hardly no space a'tall.

Your Sarah, now's a pert kind o' kid...
Young folks now days don't fancy much
This kind o' stuff...
But maybe from her grandma and
Her great aunt Hannah...

Mayhap when she's older
She'll notion to it more...

You'll see she gets it, won't you?

PURPLE

Royal purple
Struts
Postures
Pontificates
Glides on velvet
Rustles in damask
Hides in a dying
Sunset
Flashes iridescent
Off putrid flesh.

REPRIEVE

With vacant stare and sunken cheek
She lolls
Incontinent old body all akimbo
Muttering sour nothings
In her own ear.

Her chalky fingers rustle
Plucking at a coverlet
To soothe a fretful child perhaps
Or trace a lover's cheek.

"Martha, your friends are here."
Yet once again she gathers
All her meager faculties
And struggles up
Through layer upon layer
Of soft forgetfulness
To gain the aching summit
Of reality.

"John....?Sarah....?"
So obvious the effort
So taxing to sustain
That John and Sarah
Tense their bodies rigid
In sympathetic agony.

"Yes, Aunt Martha, it is us."
They stand appalled to witness
The expenditure of strength
They've caused.
"Mother sends her love,
She's sorry that she cannot come."
Now sorry that they've come themselves.

"Jennie....good...."
A further tremor of the furrowed lips
Attempted smile or something else to say
They never know.
She tumbles willy-nilly
Once again
Into the cozy comfort of oblivion.

They stand uncertainly a while
Their eyes drawn here and there
To other inmates of the room
No worse or better off
Than Martha
Though some are more aware
And here and there an eye meets theirs
In lucid comprehension.

"I guess we'd better go," says John
And Sarah nods.

They make their way among the others
To the door,
Trying not to be ashamed of walking,
Trying not to be ashamed
Of being only in their fifties.

They run the gauntlet of the corridor
With wheel chairs lined up
Flank to flank.
Guilty of their youth
They walk defenseless
Before reproachful eyes
They can go home.

They pass the kitchen
With its homely clangs
And cheerful clatter.
Roast beef must smell the same
At any age.

As last they gain the waiting room
And then outside.
They have restrained
A growing urge to run.
The smell of antiseptics and deodorants
Still clings.

They make their way in silence
To their car
And in its sanctuary
Begin to feel
Some measure of security.

"We have a few years yet," says John
And Sarah nods.

GERONTOLOGY

The web of time
Has snared another one
To dangle, withering
In the Southern sun.

Constrained to trade inanities
With other forced nonentities.

Bored and boring
In the afternoon
They speak of children, past
And children coming...soon

To verify existence
And justify persistence.

FINITY

The snow settles softly
Upon my life
And lightly lies.
Almost caressing.

I think to wear it
Graciously
But, oh, the chill
Strikes deep
Into my heart.

END OF ALL BEGINNINGS

The yesterdays of all my lives
Coalesce, and from the pool of past
Experience comes persistent, dissonant
Mutter, as of alien drums.
Each jealous cadence calls
For sole allegiance.

While down the corridor of time
I run, pursued by demons
Of remorse in common guise
Attired, treading on coals
By past mistakes and present miseries
fired. And down the hall
Tomorrow's doors
Are closing
One by one.

RECYCLED

When this quick quickness
Which quickens me of late
Apprenticeship served out
Rejoins its source, accepts another state.

How sadly, gladly then
These elements return
To earth, their source
In quick decay's slow burn.

A host become to other life
In myriad complex form
Each marvelous in itself
Unique in its own norm.

Nothing is wasted--lost
Begin to comprehend
Eternal wheels turn
With no beginning and no end.

MAY I RECALL?

May I recall
Another fall
Of asters rife in goldenrod?
May I recall sweet memories
Of energy....
And faith in God?

May I recall
A love like ours
And dreams we shared
Of endless possibilities?
May I recall a child newborn
All clothed in bright eternities
And life still good
With daily food
To fuel responsibilities?

May I recall
A job well done
And duty served
With satisfaction
And childrens' faces
All aglow
Turned to follow
Sweet attraction?

May I recall with flowing heart
Whose embers banked against the night
Still glow through ashes deep
Reflection of eternal Light?

GRACEFUL EXIT

When I am gone
And left some things undone
Fragments of dreams perhaps
Lying helter skelter

Let no one say, "Too bad
He didn't get to gather up
The tag ends of his life."

I want to go while life
Still calls me on

And love yet holds some warmth

As one who lays his toys
Aside a moment
To chase a whim
Expecting to return

But is caught up
In other things.